The Adventures of

Porcupine and His

Animal Friends

ISBN-13: 978-1-7325161-0-6
ISBN-10: 1-7325161-0-3

Front cover designed by Andrea Hansen

Image of porcupine by permission of
http://www.DailyArtHub.com

I Want to Thank

My husband Paul, who encourages me every day to keep writing and follow my dreams.

My sons Eric and Jonathon, and my daughter-in-law Andrea, who are my biggest cheerleaders.

My grandchildren Adelyn and Garrett; and my dad, who keeps telling me to write my books.

Thank you, Kathryn Holt, for your time you commit to me.

My friends for their love and support; and my students, who inspire me with their imaginations every day.

Get ready to illustrate your very own book!

You can make *The Adventures of Porcupine and His Animal Friends* come to life by using your imagination. Go on the journey with them by researching and drawing your very own pictures to illustrate each page.

My suggestion is to read the story first, then read it again and pay attention to the words and what the story is about.

Pay close attention to the characters.
A character is:

•A person, or sometimes even an animal, who takes part in the story.

In this story, the characters are animals. You need to know what kind of animals they are and what they look like.

Don't forget the setting.
The setting is:

•Where does the story take place?

•What time of the day do the different situations occur?

•What was the weather like?

•What kind of things were around them? Look for clues in the writing.

Use your imagination to make the characters and story come to life.

When you are done illustrating, you will have one of a kind book that no one else will have. How exciting is that!

Characters

Porcupine

Bear

Fox

Raccoon

Setting

Pine Trees and Mountains

"What a beautiful day in the forest today," Bear said to Raccoon and Porcupine. The pine trees had snow sitting heavily on their limbs. The sun was trying to sneak thru the high tops of the mountain clouds.

"It sure is a beautiful place," Raccoon said.

"I know," said Porcupine, "shall we play a game of Hide n' Seek?"
Everyone agreed.
"I'll hide my eyes first and count to 10," said Porcupine.
"Bear and Raccoon, you guys go and hide first."
"OK," they said. And off they went to hide.

Porcupine started to count. "1, 2, 3... 6... 8, 9, 10. OK," shouted Porcupine, "Ready or not, here I come."

Porcupine looked for Bear and Raccoon. He thought if he climbed up a tall, snow-covered pine tree he would be able to find his friends. So, that is what he did. He climbed a pine tree and looked out as far as his eyes could see, but he couldn't see or hear his friends.

Suddenly Porcupine was all alone.

"Hello," Porcupine shouted as his voice echoed throughout the forest. "Hello. Hello. Helloooooooooooo," he shouted again. He listened for his friends, Bear and Raccoon to shout "Hello" back, but all he could hear was his own voice echoing.

Porcupine ran back down the pine tree and along the icy river bank. "Bear, Raccoon," Porcupine shouted out. "Are you there? Can you hear me?" Once again he listened for his friends to shout back, but he could only hear his own voice echoing back.

Porcupine noticed it was starting to snow heavily. The snow was blowing in and around the pine trees and getting thicker on top of the mountains. The sun was beginning to set as the moon was slowly rising. It was getting dark.

Porcupine was getting worried with the darkness approaching, and hiked up the mountain. "BEAR, RACCOON," he screamed out, "I'm getting scared. Please, come out now." Again, he heard only the echo of his own voice.

Porcupine ran in and out of the snow-covered paths that were layered with deep snow. He was worried, and tried to find his way back from where he came by following his tracks.

The darkness slowly covered his tracks, making it hard for him to see, "Bearrrrrr, Raccoooooonnnnnn."
His voice was a lot quieter with the fear of knowing he was all alone.

All of a sudden....POOF.....Porcupine fell down a hole that he didn't see. He looked up and saw snowflakes falling down the hole from the sky above. The snow was glistening from the moon's light. Now he was REALLY ALONE!

"OH NO!" Porcupine thought to himself as he sat there quietly. Porcupine began to cry. He shouted in a loud voice, "My friends are NEVER going to find me now."

"Hhhmmm, hmmmmm," said a little voice behind Porcupine. Porcupine jumped up fast, not knowing where the little voice came from. "Who's there?" said Porcupine.
"Are you lost?" the little voice said behind him again. Porcupine turned around slowly, "Who's there?" said Porcupine in a frightened, quiet voice.

"It's me, Fox." As Fox leaped out from behind Porcupine, Porcupine jumped with fear. "Are…you…lost?" Fox asked again, this time with a stern voice.

"I don't know," said Porcupine who was starting to cry again. "What do you mean, you don't know? You're either lost or not lost," replied Fox.

"Well," said Porcupine, "I was playing Hide n' Seek with my friends, Bear and Raccoon, and I closed my eyes, counted to 10 and they were gone!"

"Well," said Fox, "Isn't that how you play the game?"

"Well, yes," said Porcupine, "but they were gone. I looked for them and I couldn't find them anywhere."

Porcupine continued to tell Fox, "I climbed up a tall, snow-covered pine tree to see if I could see them. Then I ran along the icy river bank, and still couldn't see them. I then ran up the mountain and in and out of the snow-covered paths, and then I fell down a hole and that's how I got here with you!"

"This isn't a hole," replied Fox, "this is my den!"

"Your den?" questioned Porcupine.

"Yes," said Fox, "this is my den, my home. This is where I live. I made my den by digging a hole in the ground like a tunnel, and I call it my den. I have a safe place to sleep and store my food."

Porcupine continued to tell Fox he was scared of being in the dark and not being able to find his friends.

"Come with me," said Fox, "let's go through the tunnel and I'll show you a way out." Porcupine agreed and started to follow Fox.

"Are you sure we are going the right way?" he asked.

"Yes," replied Fox, "keep following me."

All of a sudden, Fox came out of a hole at the end of the tunnel that led to the forest. Porcupine was behind Fox.

Bear and Raccoon saw the Fox come out of his hole along with Porcupine. Bear and Raccoon walked over to them.
"WHERE HAVE YOU BEEN?" Bear shouted to Porcupine.
"WE have been worried about you," added Raccoon.

Porcupine told them both the story of what had happened. "And then I fell down in a hole and got really, really scared, but I met Fox down there and he took me through his tunnel and showed me the way out, and here you both are."

"Well, don't EVER go off far again looking for us," said Bear, angrily. "You never know where you will find yourself in the dark," said Raccoon. "And you could be lost from us forever." "I'm sorry," said Porcupine in a quiet voice.

Bear and Raccoon looked at Fox. "Thank you for taking care of our friend," Raccoon said to Fox.
"We would be so sad if we never saw him again," said Bear.

"You are so lucky to have friends," Fox said to Porcupine.
"What do you mean?" said Porcupine to Fox.
"Well," said Fox, "I have no one! I live down in my den by myself. Like you, I am scared to be alone in the forest and that's why I built my den, to make me feel safe."

Porcupine, Bear, and Raccoon gathered around each other whispering while looking at Fox. After they had finished whispering to each other, Porcupine looked at Fox. "Well Fox," Porcupine gently said, "we are now your new friends."

"NO! REALLY!" said Fox with excitement.

"REALLY," said Bear, "we are lucky to be friends. Actually, we are more like family to each other rather than friends. Fox, do you want to be part of our family, too?"

"Oh yes, please," said Fox, joyfully jumping up and down.
"I would love a family to call my own."
And that's how the adventures began.
Off they all went together back into the forest.

"Hey, Porcupine," said Bear.
"Yes Bear," said Porcupine.
"I'm glad we found you."
"Oh, me too," said Porcupine. "Me too."

www.ingramcontent.com/pod-product-compliance
Lightning Source LLC
Chambersburg PA
CBHW041236040426
42445CB00004B/46